TRANSPORT AND TRAVEL

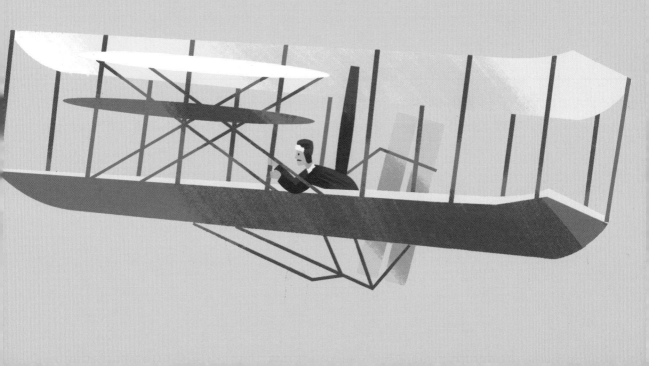

360 DEGREES
An imprint of the Little Tiger Group
1 Coda Studios, 189 Munster Road,
London SW6 6AW
www.littletiger.co.uk
First published in Great Britain 2018
Text by Sandra Lawrence
Text copyright © Sandra Lawrence 2018
Illustrated by Jem Maybank
Illustrations copyright © Jem Maybank 2018
All rights reserved • ISBN: 978-1-84857-711-4
Printed in China • CPB/1800/0866/0218
10 9 8 7 6 5 4 3 2 1

Written by Sandra Lawrence • Illustrated by Jem Maybank

TRANSPORT AND TRAVEL

INTRODUCTION

Wherever we are on the planet, we need to get around. How we travel depends on many different things. It depends on where we are and where we want to go, how far we need to travel and how fast we want to get there. We have to think about the materials available and how technology has evolved – and, of course, it depends on how much money we have!

Humans have developed hundreds of ways of moving from place to place, from riding animals across the plains to whizzing through space in powerful rockets. This book takes a voyage around the world, discovering the fastest, funkiest, flashiest and funniest ways to get where you want to go!

CONTENTS

WHEELS

The very first humans had to walk everywhere, carrying anything they needed on their backs. Sometimes they rode animals but getting from A to B was still hard work, so it's hardly surprising that the wheel was one of our ancestors' earliest inventions!

It is believed that when the mysterious monument Stonehenge was built in England over 4,000 years ago, the huge rocks may have been moved on rollers made from tree trunks. We've come a long way since then. Today, everything from suitcases to roller skates is fitted with wheels – where would we be without them?

KEEP ROLLIN' ALONG...

Every ancient army used chariots – fast-moving buggies pulled by horses – to strike terror into their enemies. Skilled charioteers would speed across the battlefield, as archers stood behind and fired arrows into the opposing ranks.

For thousands of years, carts pulled by animals carried people and their goods. When the early settlers crossed America in the 16th century, their traditional covered wagons contained everything they owned.

Gradually, chariots and carts were replaced with smarter domestic carriages that were pulled by horses. They were beautiful to look at and very expensive but also extremely uncomfortable to ride in. Less well-off people would often share the cost by riding together in a communal mail coach.

Coach and horses

Chariot

Covered wagon

ON THE BUSES

Buses are a good way to move lots of people at once. The word is short for *omnibus* which means 'for all' in Latin. Scientists have worked out that yellow is the colour the human eye most easily detects so in America, the law states that school buses *must* be that shade to keep everyone safe.

The red 'double-decker' buses of London, England, are well-known icons of the city. People visiting London for the first time often choose to sit at the front of the top deck so they can see as many sights as possible. Some double-deckers even have open tops for better views!

FLASHING LIGHTS AND SQUEALING SIRENS

Every town keeps a fleet of special vehicles ready in case there's an accident or emergency. All emergency vehicles have loud sirens and flashing lights so that people know they're coming and can get out of their way.

Ambulances are like small hospitals on wheels, so they can help people immediately. The injured person is treated by paramedics in the ambulance on their way to hospital. In busy cities, some paramedics use bicycles to whizz through traffic jams in order to reach the scene of an accident first.

An Australian ambulance

Emergency Ambulance

Fire engines have long hoses and ladders so they can put out a blaze. Many engines actually carry water on board in case there isn't a water source available when they arrive at the scene.

Police cars are able to reach high speeds in order to quickly go to wherever there is trouble. They might arrest a thief, stop people fighting or help to restore order after a traffic accident or other emergency.

A UK fire engine

An American police car

PEDAL POWER

Bicycles were invented in the late 19th century, and some of the early models were very strange-looking indeed! The penny-farthing, or high-wheeler, had one giant front wheel and a tiny rear one so the rider had to climb on top of the big wheel in order to reach the saddle!

Cycling became so popular that people didn't use bicycles just to get around, they raced them too. The most famous bicycle race in the world is the Tour de France. Every year, teams of riders race each other through the French countryside, up mountains and through cities, over 23 days. The winner of each day gets to wear a special yellow jersey and the overall winner becomes the toast of France and the world!

MOTOR-VATION

Motor cars have been with us for over 100 years. The earliest cars were very expensive because they were built by hand. In the 1920s, an American called Henry Ford started mass-producing cars in factories which made the car affordable for the first time. The Model T (*below*) was particularly popular.

By the 1950s, oil became easier to buy and cars became huge! They had sleek lines, 'fins' on the side and names like 'Thunderbird' and 'Eldorado'.

Today's cars are being designed to use less fuel so they don't pollute the environment. Electric or hybrid (fuel and electric) cars are becoming more popular and, as a result, charging stations are popping up on city streets.

NIP AND TUK-TUK

In years gone by, the rickshaw was a common vehicle on the road of many countries. These two-wheeled carts were traditionally pulled by hand, although they are now mostly driven by bicycle.

Today, especially in tropical climates, little three-wheeled vehicles called tuk-tuks do the same job. Also known as auto-rickshaws, some of these motorised vehicles are beautifully decorated to tempt pedestrians in!

RAILS

Many forms of transport run on special tracks, or rails. These can be on or in the ground and they help guide the vehicles on their journey.

Sometimes the rails are there to make the ride smoother whereas others carry an electric current inside them to power the vehicle itself. They have dedicated routes that never change and can be found all over the world – even on difficult terrains, such as steep slopes.

BUILDING UP STEAM

In the past, steam-powered engines, or locomotives, pulled train carriages. Many countries had huge networks of railways running through them, offering people the chance to travel further by land than they had ever travelled before.

Plumes of white steam puffing through countries as different as India, America and England were a common sight. Over the years, new ways of pulling carriages were invented that needed fewer engineers and ran on oil rather than coal. The new trains were easier to maintain, too.

Today, some steam trains still run as tourist attractions, but one line, which climbs Germany's Brocken Mountain, still runs a commuter service!

QUICK AS A SHOT

The Shinkansen railway network in Japan is a series of special railway lines that run very high-speed trains between cities. *Dangan ressha* or 'bullet trains' have long, pointed fronts that pierce through the air and enable the train to reach speeds of 320kmph (200mph).

These specialised trains transport more than ten billion passengers every year, and are very successful because they are so fast, clean and reliable. Even severe weather doesn't stop the service running on time – the annual average delay is 0.9 minutes, and that includes journeys through earthquakes and snowstorms!

ON THE RIGHT TRACKS

Trams, or 'streetcars', are bus-train hybrid vehicles that are often used in city centres. The tracks for trams either share road space with buses and cars or run alongside them. Road traffic has to stop for trams and oncoming trams warn pedestrians of their arrival by using a loud bell.

On some tram networks, electric cables run high in the air along the tram route. A wire device attached to the top of the tram, called a pantograph, will then make regular contact with the cables in order to power the tram.

Many German towns have tram systems with articulated trams. These are made up of segments which means they can easily go round corners.

Berlin saw the world's first electric tram line, which opened in 1881.
It was very dangerous because electricity ran through the rails in the street!

SLIP—SLIDIN' AWAY

Not all 'rails' are embedded in the ground. Blades have been used for centuries, worn by humans as ice-skates, skis or attached to carts to make sleds. Smooth blades slide really well across the ice and snow. Archaeologists have even found ice skates that are thought to be thousands of years old!

Skiing is one of the fastest non-motorised ways to get around on land and some skiers can travel faster on snow than normal cars can drive on the road! Whilst skis are mainly usually used for recreation, in some Nordic countries it is so cold that it is easier for children to ski to school than to go by car!

UP–HILL AND DOWN–TOWN

Cable cars are a system where small individual pods or cabins travel between mountains or other high places on strong aerial wires. They can also be used to transport people across rivers and wide spaces.

The famous San Francisco cable car is slightly different, as it travels on steel rails. Whilst the cabs look like small trams, they are not individually powered.

A massive underground wire pulls each cab along at a regular 14kmph (9mph). When the tram gets to the end of the line, it is turned round on a giant turntable so it faces the right way to return and repeat the journey.

TUNNEL VISION

The London Underground is more than 150 years old and is the oldest public underground railway in the world. The tunnels of the 'Tube' were originally built by cutting deep channels in the ground and then covering them over but today new tunnels are built with gigantic underground drills instead.

Tube lines cross each other and some stations host several lines so people can switch trains and travel from one side of the city to the other without ever having to surface and see daylight! In 1831, a special map was designed by a man called Harry Beck. It worked so well that all the other metro systems in the world adopted a similar design.

SCALING THE HEIGHTS

Tiny trains running on funicular railways take people up and down mountainsides and cliffs. Some, like those in Wellington, New Zealand, or Naples, Italy, can bring people to work from the suburbs in the hills.

Others installed at coastal towns, on mountains and in hilly cities are used purely for fun, taking tourists high in the air to enjoy spectacular views.

AIR

For hundreds of years humans dreamed of being able to fly but it proved too difficult. Even the famous 15th-century scientist and artist Leonardo da Vinci tried to design a flying machine but failed.

Hot air balloons eventually allowed people to take off from the ground, but powered flight has only been available for around 100 years. In that time, however, we've gone from wobbly biplanes to powerful rockets that have taken men to the Moon. Who knows what we might invent next?

CARRIED AWAY

Balloons were the first successful flying technology that could carry humans. In 1783, two French brothers called Joseph-Michel and Jacques-Étienne Montgolfier hung a basket under a giant, round bag, which they then filled with hot air. They tested the balloon by sending up a sheep, a cockerel and a duck, but kept it tethered to the ground.

Once confident in their design, the Montgolfier brothers found two brave men, a science teacher called Jean-François Pilâtre de Rozier and army officer Francois Laurent, the Marquis d'Arlandes, who agreed to take the balloon into the Paris skies. As the ropes were released the pair became the world's first ever pilots.

PLANE CRAZY

Inventing the first flying machine was an obsession shared by many and several people claimed to have built the first powered aeroplane, but in 1903, the American brothers Orville and Wilbur Wright managed to invent a plane with proper controls, so that they could steer a path through the skies.

Their craft was a biplane, so-called because it had two giant, fixed wings, one above the other, with a small cockpit in the middle for someone to sit in. Within ten years, the aviation industry was big business and flying humans were here to stay.

SONIC BOOM

Today, most commercial planes are jet-powered. Unlike early, propeller-driven aeroplanes, jet engines pull air in then force it out as a jet of hot exhaust, which, in turn, shoots the aircraft through the sky. As a result, jet areoplanes can move at very high speeds.

Some supersonic planes can go faster than the speed of sound. When they hit the sound barrier, supersonic planes make a loud bang called a sonic boom. There used to be one commercial supersonic plane, called Concorde, but it was very expensive to run and didn't take many passengers for its size and power. Nowadays we have giant 'jumbo' jets that carry lots of people – and even bigger planes are on the way.

ROTOR—VATION

Helicopters have blades called rotors that spin round very fast to keep the craft in the air. They are very agile vehicles and can take off and land without a runway. Helicopters can also hover in one spot, which makes them excellent for rescuing people who have got into trouble in the sea, in remote places and, especially, on mountainsides.

Helicopters also have powerful lamps that provide enough light to search for lost mountaineers on the ground and crew members are often winched down to administer first aid. Patients can then be carried straight to safety and, if they need medical attention, to hospital as many hospitals have landing facilities or 'helipads' on their roofs.

THE FINAL FRONTIER

Once humans had conquered taking off into the clouds, it wasn't long before their attention was drawn to the stars. In the 20th century, a huge amount of funding was put into advancing space technology around the world and scientists and astronauts began to push the limits of space travel further and further by harnessing the power of rockets.

Rocket engines work using chemical reactions to generate enough pressure and power to blast them up into the sky. In 1969, astronaut Neil Armstrong was the first human to walk on the Moon and since then we have launched unmanned spacecraft, like the Mars rover, further into space in order to uncover the secrets of the stars and planets.

FUTURE–PROVING

For many people the ideal way to fly would be by using a device that propels you into the air, without having to be confined in a machine.

People have been experimenting with 'jet packs' – a rucksack-like device that will allow a person to fly – for many years. Some are able to take humans up in the air but only for very short periods of time. They can be useful in space for space-walks but they are not yet practical enough to use on Earth.

WATER

Over 70% of the Earth is covered by water, so it's not surprising that humans have been finding ways to travel across it since ancient times. The very first boats would have been hollowed-out tree trunks or logs tied to make rafts, moved with paddles or long poles.

Today, we love water more than ever, whether it's shooting rapids in single-person kayaks or lounging in vast cruise liners that are more like floating cities than the ships of our ancestors.

PILLAGE, PLUNDER
AND PLAIN SAILING

The Norsemen, who we often call Vikings, came from Northern Europe between 1,000 and 1,300 years ago. They were great seafarers and travelled in longships (very fast sailing boats designed for quick raids).

Longships were very narrow, which meant they could continue up fjords and rivers. They were also double-ended, so if things didn't go well, the Vikings could hop back in and sail away without needing to turn round!

Longships were sometimes called 'dragon ships' because of the carved dragon's head at the front which was meant to scare off sea monsters.

MASTS AND MAINSAILS

Many people call the time between the late 16th century and the mid-19th century the Age of Sail. It was the era of the tall ships – giant wooden boats with tall masts and massive sails. Some were merchant vessels, carrying valuable goods to sell, whilst others belonged to the navy, who were often looking out for people with an eye for tall ships: pirates.

The Chinese 'junk' is a different kind of sailing ship, known mainly in the Far East. It travels low in the water and its sails are much simpler than western rigging, while still being very versatile. Junks are fast and stable and they can be ocean-going ships or small pleasure craft. They are still used today, mainly by fishermen.

OAR-SOME

Traditional Native American canoes have changed very little from the earliest boats and some of the oldest examples we have today are over 1,000 years old. Some are hollow tree trunks, others are made from light wood, bark or stretched animal hide. They were all different so tribes could recognise who was travelling by the shape and style of their canoe.

In South America traditional canoes were often made from reeds tightly tied together. Though most people use modern materials, such as fibreglass, polythene and even aluminium when building canoes today, classic wooden canoes are still popular and used for exhibitions and festivals.

CANAL ROUTES

The city of Venice, known as the 'Floating City', sits across 118 small islands and its 'streets' are actually canals. To get around, the people traditionally used to use *gondolas*. These black, flat-bottomed boats were steered with large, loose oars by *gondoliers*. In their heyday, the 17th and 18th centuries, it was said gondoliers knew everything that was going on in the city, from all the gossip they heard in their boats!

Today, most locals travel by water taxi, or *vaporettos*, but there are still around 400 gondoliers working on the canals who wear the traditional striped top, red scarf and straw hat and take visitors on sightseeing trips around the city. It is still a very special treat to travel by gondola.

SHOWBOATS AND WATER PALACES

Like trains, some ships used to be driven by steam. Paddle steamers have huge wheels at the back with paddles on them that constantly churn the water and, as the wheels turn, the ship is propelled forward. Some 'paddlers' were capable of crossing oceans, but the most famous ones travelled up and down the Mississippi River during the 19th century.

These paddle steamers were very luxurious, like palaces on water and some, called 'showboats', even had theatres on board. People might travel on them, or just turn up when the boat docked to enjoy an evening's entertainment. There are still some paddle steamers operating today.

WALKING ON WATER

Hovercrafts create cushions of air underneath them which allow them to glide across the surface of water. The air is held in by a large 'skirt', which means that the craft doesn't have to spend energy ploughing through the waves, it glides over the water instead.

The giant propellers on the back of the hovercraft add to the speed – with hovercrafts being able to travel at up to 145kmph (90mph). Most forms of transport are designed to travel over one sort of surface but hovercrafts happily shoot across any combination of ice, water, snow, mud and sand.

DOWN UNDER

Submarines don't just move *through* the water, they can stealthily move *under* the water as well.

They are specially pressurised vehicles that can dive to incredible depths as well as maintain an environment where a crew is able to live safely on board.

Submarines have periscopes that can stick up out of the water so the crew can see what's going on above the surface. Submarines are often used by naval crews but not always for war. They are useful for underwater repairs to cables, archaeology, marine science and for salvaging shipwrecks.

RACING THE WAVES

Some speedboats are just small vessels with an attached engine called an outboard motor. Others, called Rigid Inflatable Boats, or RIBs, are made very fast and light by their inflatable hulls.

They are used by lots of different people, from the police to rescue teams, but lots of people keep RIBs as pleasure boats and some even race them.

Sometimes people wear water skis to skim over the surface of the ocean. They are pulled along behind a speedboat for an exciting ride!

Jet skis are a bit like motorbikes for the water. They are very fast and can carry one or two passengers at a time.

SAVE OUR SOULS

In coastal communities around the world, from Great Britain to Brazil and from Uruguay to Kenya, there are very special groups of people who, as well as managing day jobs, also volunteer as part of a lifeboat rescue crew.

Volunteer lifeboat crews are highly trained and ready to be called at any hour of the day or night, so they can rescue people who find themselves in trouble at sea. The lifeboats are light and easy to move, yet tough enough to face storms and have saved many hundreds of lives.